Recipes from a
Country Kitchen

Recipes from a
Country Kitchen

LIZ TRIGG

Photographs by Michelle Garrett

SMITHMARK

This edition published in 1996 by
SMITHMARK Publishers
a division of U.S. Media Holdings, Inc.,
16 East 32nd Street
New York, NY 10016

SMITHMARK books are available for bulk purchase, for sales promotion and
for premium use. For details, write or call the manager of special sales,
SMITHMARK Publishers, 16 East 32nd Street,
New York, NY 10016; (212) 532–6600

10 9 8 7 6 5 4 3 2

ISBN 0-7651-9839-8

Publisher: Joanna Lorenz
Project editor: Sarah Ainley
Designer: Janet James
Photographer: Michelle Garrett
Illustrator: Nadine Wickenden
Recipes pp. 8, 9, 16, 17, 30, 31, 48, 49 by Andi Clevely and Katherine Richmond
Additional photography by John Freeman

Printed in Singapore by Star Standard Industries Pte. Ltd.

Contents

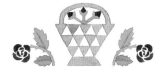

Spring Recipes

....

Spring brings the first of the year's tender young vegetables, and there are plenty of tempting recipes to make the most of seasonal produce. Treat yourself to a zesty lemon cake or an Easter bread studded with fruit and spices, for an Easter breakfast.

Pear and Watercress Soup with Stilton Croûtons

Pears and Stilton taste very good when you eat them together after the main course – here, for a change, they are served as a starter.

INGREDIENTS

1 bunch watercress
4 medium pears, sliced
3¾ cups chicken stock, preferably home-made
salt and pepper
½ cup heavy cream
juice of 1 lime

Croûtons
2 tbsp butter
1 tbsp olive oil
3 cups cubed stale bread
1 cup chopped Stilton cheese

Serves 6

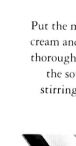

1

Keep back about a third of the watercress leaves. Place all the rest of the watercress leaves and stalks in a pan with the pears, stock and a little seasoning. Simmer for about 15–20 minutes. Reserving some watercress leaves for garnishing, add the rest of the leaves and immediately blend in a food processor until smooth.

2

Put the mixture into a bowl and stir in the cream and the lime juice to mix the flavors thoroughly. Season again to taste. Pour all the soup back into a pan and reheat, stirring gently until warmed through.

3

To make the croûtons, melt the butter and oil and fry the bread cubes until golden brown. Drain on paper towels. Put the cheese on top and heat under a hot grill until bubbling. Reheat the soup and pour into bowls. Divide the croûtons and remaining watercress between the bowls.

Spinach, Cognac, Garlic and Chicken Pâté

*Pâté is an easy starter, as it can be made well in advance. This smooth version
is delicious with warm brown rolls and butter or garlic bread.*

INGREDIENTS

*12 slices lean bacon
2 tbsp butter
1 onion, peeled and chopped
1 clove garlic, peeled and crushed
10 oz frozen spinach, thawed
¾ cup finely crumbled whole
wheat bread
2 tbsp Cognac
1 lb ground chicken (dark and
light meat)
1 lb ground pork
2 eggs, beaten
2 tbsp chopped mixed fresh herbs,
such as parsley, sage and dill
salt and pepper*

Serves 12

1

Fry the bacon in a pan until it is only just
done, then arrange it round the sides of a
1 quart ovenproof loaf pan, if possible
leaving a couple of slices to garnish.

3

Preheat the oven to 350°F. Combine all the
remaining ingredients, apart from any
remaining bacon strips, in a bowl and mix
well to blend. Spoon the pâté into the loaf
pan and cover with any remaining bacon.

2

Melt the butter in a pan. Fry the onion and
garlic until soft. Squeeze the spinach to
remove as much water as possible, then add
to the pan, stirring until the spinach is dry.

4

Cover the pan with a double thickness of foil
and set it in a baking pan. Pour 1 in boiling
water into the baking pan. Bake for about
1¼ hours. Remove the pâté and let it cool.
Place a heavy weight on top of the pâté
and refrigerate overnight.

Spring Roasted Chicken with Fresh Herbs and Garlic

A smaller chicken or four squabs can also be roasted in this way.

INGREDIENTS

*4½ lb free-range chicken or
4 small squabs
finely grated rind and
juice of 1 lemon
1 garlic clove, crushed
2 tbsp olive oil
2 fresh thyme sprigs
2 fresh sage sprigs
6 tbsp unsalted butter,
softened
salt and freshly ground
black pepper*

Serves 4

1

Season the chicken or squabs well.
Mix the lemon rind and juice, garlic and
olive oil together and pour them over the
chicken. Leave to marinate for at least
2 hours in a non-metallic dish.
When the chicken has marinated preheat
the oven to 450°F.

2

Place the herbs in the cavity of the bird and
smear the butter over the skin. Season well.
Roast the chicken for 10 minutes, then turn
the oven down to 375°F. Baste the chicken
well, and then roast for a further 1 hour
30 minutes, until the juices run clear when
the thigh is pierced with a skewer. Leave to
rest for 15 minutes before carving.

Lemon and Rosemary Lamb Chops

*Spring lamb is delicious with the fresh flavor of lemon. Garnish with sprigs of
fresh rosemary – the aroma is irresistible.*

INGREDIENTS

*12 lamb chops
3 tbsp olive oil
2 large rosemary sprigs
juice of 1 lemon
3 garlic cloves, sliced
salt and freshly ground
black pepper*

Serves 4

1

Trim the excess fat from the chops.
Mix the oil, rosemary, lemon juice and
garlic together and season well.
Preheat the broiler.

2

Pour over the chops in a shallow dish and
marinate for 30 minutes. Remove from the
marinade, and blot the excess with kitchen
paper and broil for 10 minutes on each side.

Carrot and Cilantro Soufflés

Use tender young carrots for this light-as-air dish.

INGREDIENTS

1 lb carrots
2 tbsp fresh chopped
cilantro
4 eggs, separated
salt and freshly ground
black pepper

Serves 4

1

Peel the carrots.

2

Cook in boiling salted water for 20 minutes or until tender. Drain, and process until smooth in a food processor.

3

Preheat the oven to 400°F. Season the puréed carrots well, and stir in the chopped cilantro.

4

Fold the egg yolks into the carrot mixture.

5

In a separate bowl, whisk the egg whites until stiff.

6

Fold the egg whites into the carrot mixture and pour into four greased ramekins. Bake for about 20 minutes or until risen and golden. Serve immediately.

Leeks with Ham and Cheese Sauce

A tasty lunch or supper dish: use a strong cheese for best results.

INGREDIENTS

4 leeks
4 slices ham

For the sauce
2 tbsp unsalted butter
1 tbsp all-purpose flour
1 ¼ cups milk
½ tsp French mustard
4 oz Cheddar cheese, grated
salt and freshly ground
black pepper

Serves 4

1

Preheat the oven to 375°F. Trim the leeks to 1 in of the white and cook in salted water for about 20 minutes until soft. Drain thoroughly. Wrap the leeks in the ham slices.

2

To make the sauce, melt the butter in a saucepan. Add the flour and cook for a few minutes. Remove from the heat and gradually add the milk, whisking well with each addition. Return to the heat and whisk until the sauce thickens. Stir in the mustard and 3 oz of the cheese and season well. Lay the leeks in a shallow ovenproof dish and pour the sauce over. Scatter the extra cheese on top and bake for 20 minutes.

Baked Eggs with Heavy Cream and Chives

This is a rich dish best served with Melba toast: it's very easy and quick to make.

INGREDIENTS

1 tbsp unsalted butter,
softened
4 tbsp heavy cream
1 tbsp chopped fresh chives
4 eggs
2 oz Gruyère cheese,
finely grated
salt and freshly ground
black pepper

Serves 2

1

Preheat the oven to 350°F. Grease two individual gratin dishes. Mix the cream with the chives, and season with salt and pepper.

2

Break the eggs into each dish and top with the cream mixture. Sprinkle the cheese around the edges of the dishes and bake in the oven for 15–20 minutes. When cooked, brown the tops under the broiler for a minute.

Zucchini and Carrot Ribbons with Brie, Black Pepper and Parsley

This recipe produces a delicious vegetarian meal, or simply a new way of presenting colorful vegetables as an accompaniment to a main course.

INGREDIENTS

1 large green pepper, diced
1 tbsp sunflower oil
8 oz Brie cheese
2 tbsp plain yogurt
1 tsp lemon juice
4 tbsp milk
2 tsp freshly ground black pepper
2 tbsp parsley, very finely
chopped, plus extra to garnish
salt and pepper
6 large zucchini
6 large carrots

Serves 4

1

Sauté the green pepper in the sunflower oil until just tender. Place the remaining ingredients, apart from the carrots and zucchini, in a food processor and blend well. Place the mixture in a saucepan and add the green pepper.

2

Peel the zucchini. Use a potato peeler to slice them into long, thin strips. Do the same thing with the carrots. Put the zucchini and carrots in separate saucepans, cover with just enough water to cover, then simmer for 3 minutes until barely cooked.

3

Heat the sauce and pour into a shallow vegetable dish. Toss the zucchini and carrot strips together and arrange them in the sauce. Garnish with a little finely chopped parsley.

Stuffed Tomatoes, with Wild Rice, Corn and Cilantro

These tomatoes could be served as a light meal with crusty bread and a salad, or as an accompaniment to most meats or fish.

INGREDIENTS

8 medium tomatoes
1/3 cup corn kernels
2 tbsp white wine
1/4 cup cooked wild rice
1 clove garlic
1/2 cup grated sharp Cheddar cheese
1 tbsp chopped fresh cilantro
salt and pepper
1 tbsp olive oil

Serves 4

1

Cut the tops off the tomatoes and remove the seeds with a small teaspoon. Scoop out all the flesh and chop finely – also chop the tops.

2

Preheat the oven to 350°F. Put the chopped tomato in a pan. Add the corn and the white wine. Cover with a close-fitting lid and simmer until tender. Drain.

3

Mix together all the remaining ingredients except the olive oil, adding salt and pepper to taste. Carefully spoon the mixture into the tomatoes, piling it higher in the center. Sprinkle the oil over the top, arrange the tomatoes in an ovenproof dish, and bake at 350°F for 15–20 minutes until cooked through.

Lemon Drizzle Cake

You can also make this recipe using a large orange instead of the lemons;
either way, it makes a zesty treat for afternoon tea.

INGREDIENTS

finely grated rind of 2 lemons
¾ cup superfine sugar
1 cup unsalted butter,
softened
4 eggs
2 cups self-rising flour
1 tsp baking powder
¼ tsp salt
shredded rind of 1 lemon,
and 1 tsp granulated sugar
to decorate

For the syrup
juice of 1 lemon
¾ cup superfine sugar

Serves 6

1

Preheat the oven to 325°F. Grease a 2 lb loaf pan or 7–8 in round cake pan and line it with wax paper or baking parchment. Mix the lemon rind and superfine sugar together.

2

Cream the butter with the lemon and sugar mixture. Add the eggs and mix until smooth. Sift the flour, baking powder and salt into a bowl and fold a third at a time into the mixture. Turn the batter into the pan, smooth the top and bake for 1½ hours or until golden brown and springy to the touch.

3

To make the syrup, slowly heat the juice with the sugar and dissolve it gently. Make several slashes in the top of the cake and pour the syrup over. Sprinkle the shredded lemon rind and 1 tsp granulated sugar on top and leave to cool.

Whole Wheat Bread

Homemade bread creates one of the most evocative smells in country cooking.
Eat this on the day you bake it, to enjoy the superb fresh taste.

INGREDIENTS

¾ oz fresh yeast
1¼ cups lukewarm milk
1 tsp superfine sugar
1½ cups whole wheat flour,
sifted
2 cups all-purpose white flour,
sifted
1 tsp salt
4 tbsp butter, chilled and cubed
1 egg, lightly beaten
2 tbsp mixed seeds

Makes 4 round loaves or
2 long loaves

1

Gently dissolve the yeast with a little of the milk and the sugar to make a paste. Place both the flours plus any bran from the sifter and the salt in a large warmed mixing bowl. Rub in the butter until the mixture resembles bread crumbs.

2

Add the yeast mixture, remaining milk and egg and mix into a fairly soft dough. Knead on a floured board for 15 minutes. Lightly grease the mixing bowl and put the dough back in the bowl, covering it with a piece of greased plastic wrap. Let rise until double in size in a warm place (this should take at least an hour).

3

Punch the dough down and knead it for a further 10 minutes. Preheat the oven to 400°F. To make round loaves, divide the dough into four pieces and shape them into flattish rounds. Place them on a floured baking sheet and let rise for a further 15 minutes. Sprinkle the loaves with the mixed seeds. Bake for about 20 minutes until golden and firm.

NOTE

For pan-shaped loaves, put the punched-down dough into two greased loaf pans instead. Let rise for a further 45 minutes and then bake for about 45 minutes, until the loaf sounds hollow when turned out of the pan and knocked on the base.

Easter Braid

Serve this delicious bread sliced with butter and jam.
It is also very good toasted on the day after you made it.

INGREDIENTS

⅞ cup milk
2 eggs, lightly beaten
6 tbsp superfine sugar
4 cups all-purpose flour
½ tsp salt
2 tsp ground allspice
6 tbsp butter
¾ oz fresh yeast

1¼ cups currants
¼ cup candied mixed citrus
peel, chopped
a little sweetened milk, to glaze
1½ tbsp candied cherries,
chopped
1 tbsp angelica, chopped

Serves 8

1

Warm the milk to lukewarm, add two-thirds of it to the eggs and mix in the sugar.

2

Sift the flour, salt and allspice together. Rub in the butter. Make a well in the center of the flour, add the milk and yeast, adding more milk as necessary to make a sticky dough.

3

Knead on a well-floured surface and then knead in the currants and mixed peel, reserving 1 tbsp for the topping. Put the dough in a lightly greased bowl and cover it with a damp dish towel. Let rise until double its size. Preheat the oven to 425°F.

4

Turn the dough out on to a floured surface and knead again for 2–3 minutes. Divide the dough into three even pieces. Roll each piece into a sausage shape roughly 8 in long. Braid the three pieces together, turning under and pinching each end. Place on a floured baking sheet and let rise for 15 minutes.

5

Brush the top with sweetened milk and scatter with coarsely chopped cherries, strips of angelica and the reserved peel. Bake in the preheated oven for 45 minutes or until the bread sounds hollow when tapped on the bottom. Cool slightly on a wire rack.

Orange-blossom Mold

A fresh orange gelatin mold makes a delightful dessert: the natural fruit flavor combined with the smooth gelatin has a clean taste that is especially welcome after a rich main course. This is delicious served with thin, crisp cookies.

INGREDIENTS

5 tbsp superfine sugar
²/₃ cup water
2 packets of gelatin
(about 1 oz)
2¹/₂ cups freshly squeezed
orange juice
2 tbsp orange-flower water

Serves 4–6

1

Place the superfine sugar and water in a small saucepan and gently heat to dissolve the sugar. Leave to cool.

2

Sprinkle the gelatin over ensuring it is completely dissolved in the water. Let stand until the gelatin has absorbed all the liquid and is solid.

3

Gently melt the gelatin over a bowl of simmering water until it becomes clear and transparent. Leave to cool. When the gelatin is cold, mix it with the orange juice and orange-flower water.

4

Wet a mold and pour in the gelatin. Chill in the refrigerator for at least 2 hours, or until set. Turn out to serve.

Rhubarb and Orange Crumble

The almonds give this crumble topping a nutty taste and crunchy texture.
This crumble is extra-delicious with home-made custard.

INGREDIENTS

2 lb rhubarb, cut in
2 in lengths
6 tbsp superfine sugar
finely grated rind and juice
of 2 oranges

1 cup all-purpose flour
½ cup unsalted butter,
chilled and cubed
6 tbsp demerara sugar
1¼ cups ground almonds

Serves 6

1

Preheat the oven to 350°F. Place the rhubarb
in a shallow ovenproof dish.

2

Sprinkle the superfine sugar over and add the
orange rind and juice.

3

Sift the flour into a mixing bowl and add the
butter. Rub the butter into the flour until
the mixture resembles bread crumbs.

4

Add the demerara sugar and ground almonds
and mix well.

5

Spoon the crumble mixture over the fruit to
cover it completely. Bake for 40 minutes,
until the top is browned and the fruit is
cooked. Serve warm.

Summer Recipes

The warm, lazy days and long nights of summer
provide the perfect excuse for outdoor dining
with friends and family. Try Mediterranean quiche
or a glorious garden salad with nasturtium flowers.
Cooling treats include strawberry fool, or
homemade mint ice cream.

Mackerel with Roasted Blueberries

Fresh blueberries burst with flavor when roasted, and their sharpness complements the rich flesh of mackerel very well.

INGREDIENTS

2 tsp all-purpose flour
4 small cooked, smoked mackerel
4 tbsp unsalted butter
juice of ½ lemon
salt and freshly ground
black pepper

For the roasted blueberries
1 lb blueberries
2 tbsp superfine sugar
1 tbsp unsalted butter
salt and freshly ground
black pepper

Serves 4

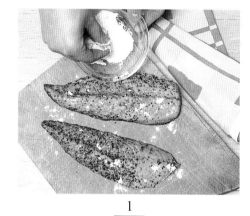

1

Preheat the oven to 400°F. Season the flour. Dip each fish fillet into the flour to coat it well.

2

Dot the butter on the fillets and bake in the oven for 20 minutes.

3

Place the blueberries, sugar, butter and seasoning in a separate small roasting pan and roast them, basting them occasionally, for 15 minutes. To serve, drizzle the lemon juice over the roasted mackerel, accompanied by the roasted blueberries.

Pan-fried Trout with Bacon

This dish can also be cooked under the broiler.

INGREDIENTS

1 tbsp all-purpose flour
4 trout, cleaned and gutted
3 oz lean bacon
4 tbsp butter
1 tbsp olive oil
juice of ½ lemon
salt and freshly ground
black pepper

Serves 4

1

Pat the trout dry with paper towels and
mix the flour and seasoning together.

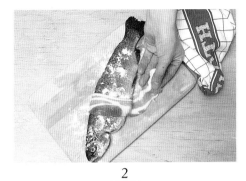

2

Roll the trout in the seasoned flour mixture
and wrap tightly in the bacon. Heat a
heavy frying pan. Heat the butter and
oil in the pan and fry the trout for 5 minutes
on each side. Serve immediately, with the
lemon juice drizzled on top.

Lamb Steaks Marinated in Mint and Sherry

The marinade is the key to the success of this recipe. The sherry imparts a wonderful tang.

INGREDIENTS

6 large lamb steaks or 12 smaller chops

Marinade
2 tbsp chopped fresh mint leaves
1 tbsp cracked black peppercorns
1 medium onion, chopped
½ cup sherry
¼ cup extra virgin olive oil
2 cloves garlic

Serves 6

1

Place the mint leaves and peppercorns in a food processor and blend until very finely chopped. Add the chopped onion and process again until smooth. Add the rest of the marinade ingredients and process until completely mixed. The marinade should be of a fairly thick consistency.

2

Place the steaks or chops in a shallow dish and pour on the marinade. Cover with plastic wrap and refrigerate overnight.

3

Broil or barbecue the steaks on a very high heat until cooked, basting occasionally with the marinade.

Broccoli and Cauliflower with a Cider and Apple Mint Sauce

The cider sauce made here is also ideal for other vegetables, such as celery or beans. It is flavored using tamari, a Japanese soy sauce, and apple mint.

INGREDIENTS

1 large onion, chopped
2 large carrots, chopped
1 large clove garlic
1 tbsp dill seed
4 large sprigs apple mint
2 tbsp olive oil
2 tbsp plain flour
1¼ cups dry cider
1 lb broccoli florets
1 lb cauliflower florets
2 tbsp tamari
2 tsp mint jelly

Serves 4

1

Sauté the onions, carrots, garlic, dill seeds and apple mint leaves in the olive oil until nearly cooked. Stir in the flour and cook for half a minute or so. Pour in the cider and simmer until the sauce looks glossy.

2

Boil the broccoli and cauliflower in separate pots until just tender.

3

Pour the sauce into a food processor and add the tamari and the mint jelly. Blend until finely puréed. Pour over the broccoli and cauliflower.

Mediterranean Quiche

*The strong Mediterranean flavors of tomatoes, peppers and anchovies
beautifully complement the cheese pastry in this unusual quiche.*

INGREDIENTS

For the pastry
2 cups all-purpose flour
pinch of salt
pinch of mustard
*½ cup butter, chilled and
cubed*
2 oz Gruyère cheese, grated

For the filling
*2 oz can of anchovies in oil,
drained*
¼ cup milk
2 tbsp French mustard
3 tbsp olive oil
*2 large Spanish onions, peeled
and sliced*
*1 red bell pepper, seeded and
very finely sliced*
3 egg yolks
1½ cups heavy cream
1 garlic clove, crushed
*6 oz sharp Cheddar
cheese, grated*
2 large tomatoes, thickly sliced
*salt and freshly ground
black pepper*
*2 tbsp chopped fresh basil,
to garnish*

Serves 12

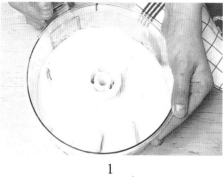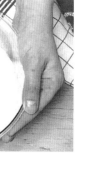

1

First make the pastry. Place the flour, salt
and mustard in a food processor,
add the butter and process the mixture
until it resembles bread crumbs.

2

Add the cheese and process again briefly.
Add enough iced water to make a stiff
dough: it will be ready when the dough
forms a ball. Wrap with plastic wrap and
chill for 30 minutes.

3

Meanwhile, make the filling. Soak the
anchovies in the milk for 20 minutes.
Pour off the milk.

4

Roll out the chilled pastry and line a 9 in
loose-based quiche pan. Spread the mustard
over and chill for a further 15 minutes.

5

Preheat the oven to 400°F. Heat the oil in a
frying pan and cook the onions and red
pepper until soft. In a separate bowl, beat
the egg yolks, cream, garlic and Cheddar
cheese together; season well. Arrange the
tomatoes in a single layer in the pastry crust.
Top with the onion and pepper mixture
and the anchovy fillets. Pour the egg
mixture over. Bake for 30–35 minutes.
Sprinkle over the basil and serve.

New Potato Salad

Potatoes freshly dug up from the garden are the best. Always leave the skins on: just wash the dirt away thoroughly. If you add the mayonnaise and other ingredients when the potatoes are hot, the flavors will develop as the potatoes cool.

INGREDIENTS

2 lb baby new potatoes
2 green apples, cored and chopped
4 scallions, chopped
3 celery stalks, finely chopped
²/₃ cup homemade or storebought
mayonnaise
salt and freshly ground
black pepper

Serves 6

1

Cook the potatoes in salted, boiling water for about 20 minutes, or until they are very tender.

2

Drain the potatoes well and immediately add the remaining ingredients and stir until well mixed. Let cool and serve cold.

Green Bean Salad

The secret of this recipe is to dress the beans while still hot.

INGREDIENTS

6 oz cherry tomatoes,
halved
1 tsp sugar
1 lb green beans, topped
and tailed
6 oz feta cheese, cubed
salt and freshly ground
black pepper

For the dressing
6 tbsp olive oil
3 tbsp white-wine vinegar
¼ tsp Dijon mustard
2 garlic cloves, crushed
salt and freshly ground
black pepper

Serves 6

1

Preheat the oven to 450°F. Put the cherry tomatoes on a baking sheet and sprinkle the sugar, salt and pepper over. Roast for 20 minutes, then let cool. Meanwhile, cook the beans in boiling salted water for 10 minutes.

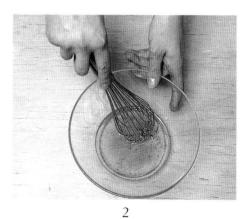

2

Make the dressing by whisking together the oil, vinegar, mustard, garlic and seasoning. Drain the beans and immediately pour the vinaigrette over and mix well. When cool, stir in the roasted tomatoes and the feta cheese. Serve chilled.

Squash à la Greque

A traditional French-style dish that is usually made with mushrooms.
Make sure that you cook the baby squash until they are quite tender,
so they can fully absorb the delicious flavors of the marinade.

INGREDIENTS

6 oz pattypan squash
1 cup white wine
juice of 2 lemons
fresh thyme sprig
bay leaf
small bunch of fresh chervil,
coarsely chopped
¼ tsp coriander seeds, crushed
¼ tsp black peppercorns, crushed
5 tbsp olive oil

Serves 4

__1__

Blanch the pattypan squash in boiling
water for 3 minutes, and then refresh them
in cold water.

__2__

Place all the remaining ingredients in a pan,
add ⅔ cup of water and simmer for 10
minutes, covered. Add the patty pans and
cook for 10 minutes. Remove with a slotted
spoon when they are cooked and tender
to the bite.

__3__

Reduce the liquid by boiling hard for
10 minutes. Strain it and pour it over the
squashes. Leave until cool for the flavors to
be absorbed. Serve cold.

Garden Salad

You can use any fresh, edible flowers from your garden for this beautiful salad.

INGREDIENTS

1 Romaine lettuce
6 oz arugula
1 small frisée lettuce
fresh chervil and tarragon sprigs
1 tbsp chopped fresh chives
handful of mixed edible flower
heads, such as nasturtiums
or marigolds

For the dressing
3 tbsp olive oil
1 tbsp white-wine vinegar
½ tsp French mustard
1 garlic clove, crushed
pinch of sugar

Serves 4

1

Mix the Romaine, arugula and frisée leaves and herbs together.

2

Make the dressing by whisking all the ingredients together in a large bowl. Toss the salad leaves in the bowl with the dressing, add the flower heads and serve at once.

Country Strawberry Fool

Make this delicious fool on the day you want to eat it, and chill it well, for the best strawberry taste.

INGREDIENTS

1 ¼ cups milk
2 egg yolks
scant ½ cup superfine sugar
few drops of vanilla extract
2 lb ripe strawberries, stemmed and washed
juice of ½ lemon
1 ¼ cups heavy cream

To decorate
12 small strawberries
4 fresh mint sprigs

Serves 4

1

First make the custard. Whisk 2 tbsp milk with the egg yolks, 1 tbsp superfine sugar and the vanilla extract.

2

Heat the remaining milk until it is just below boiling point.

3

Stir the milk into the egg mixture. Rinse the pan out and return the mixture to it.

4

Gently heat and stir until the custard thickens enough to coat the back of a wooden spoon. Lay a wet piece of wax paper on the top of the custard and let it cool.

5

Purée the strawberries in a food processor or blender with the lemon juice and the remaining sugar.

6

Lightly whip the cream and fold in the fruit purée and custard. Pour into glass dishes and decorate with the whole strawberries and sprigs of mint.

Mint Ice Cream

*This ice cream is best served slightly softened, so take it out
of the freezer 20 minutes before you want to serve it. For a special occasion,
this looks spectacular served in an ice bowl.*

INGREDIENTS

8 egg yolks
6 tbsp superfine sugar
2½ cups light cream
1 vanilla bean
4 tbsp chopped fresh mint,
to garnish

Serves 8

1

Beat the egg yolks and sugar until they are
pale and light using a hand-held electric
beater or a balloon whisk. Transfer to a
small saucepan.

2

In a separate saucepan, bring the cream to
a boil with the vanilla bean.

3

Remove the vanilla bean and pour the
hot cream on to the egg mixture,
whisking briskly.

4

Continue whisking to ensure the eggs
are mixed into the cream.

5

Gently heat the mixture until the custard
thickens enough to coat the back of a
wooden spoon. Let cool.

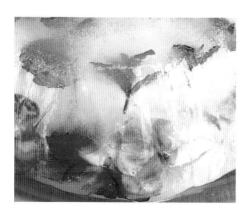

6

Stir in the mint and place in an ice-cream
maker to churn, about 3–4 hours. If you
don't have an ice-cream maker, freeze the
ice cream until mushy and then whisk it well
again, to break down the ice crystals. Freeze
for another 3 hours until it is softly frozen
and whisk again. Finally freeze until hard:
at least 6 hours.

Mixed Berry Tart

The orange-flavored pastry is delicious with the fresh fruits of summer.
Serve this with some extra shreds of orange rind scattered on top.

INGREDIENTS

For the pastry
2 cups all-purpose flour
½ cup unsalted butter
finely grated rind of 1 orange,
plus extra to decorate

For the filling
1¼ cups crème fraîche
and ¾ cup whipped cream
or ¾ cup sour cream
finely grated rind of 1 lemon
2 tsp confectioner's sugar
1½ lb mixed summer
berries

Serves 8

1

To make the pastry, put the flour and butter in a large bowl. Rub in the butter until the mixture resembles bread crumbs.

2

Add the orange rind and enough cold water to make a soft dough.

3

Roll into a ball and chill for at least 30 minutes. Roll out the pastry on a lightly floured surface.

4

Line a 9 in loose-based quiche pan with the pastry. Chill for 30 minutes. Preheat the oven to 400°F and place a baking sheet in the oven to heat up. Line the pan with wax paper and baking beans and bake blind on the baking sheet for 15 minutes. Remove the paper and beans and bake for 10 minutes more, until the pastry is golden. Allow to cool completely. To make the filling, whisk the crème fraîche, lemon rind and sugar together and pour into the pastry crust. Top with fruit, sprinkle with orange rind and serve sliced.

Autumn Recipes

*Reap the benefits of the autumn harvest with this
collection of recipes; wild mushroom tart,
thyme-roasted onions and duck and chestnut casserole
all make the most of autumn produce.
Warming desserts such as steamed ginger and
syrup pudding, or poached pears, are guaranteed to
keep away the autumn chill.*

Wild Mushroom Tart

The flavor of wild mushrooms makes this tart really rich: use as wide a variety of mushrooms as you can get.

INGREDIENTS

For the pastry
2 cups all-purpose flour
4 tbsp Crisco
2 tsp lemon juice
about ⅔ cup ice water
½ cup butter, chilled and cubed
1 egg, beaten, to glaze

For the filling
10 tbsp butter
2 shallots, finely chopped
2 garlic cloves, crushed
1 lb mixed wild mushrooms such as porcini, oyster mushrooms, or shiitake mushrooms, sliced
3 tbsp chopped fresh parsley
2 tbsp heavy cream
salt and freshly ground black pepper

Serves 6

___1___

To make the pastry, sift the flour and ½ tsp salt together into a large bowl. Add the Crisco and rub into the mixture until it resembles bread crumbs.

___2___

Add the lemon juice and enough ice water to make a soft but not sticky dough. Cover and chill for 20 minutes.

___3___

Roll the pastry out into a rectangle on a lightly floured surface. Mark the dough into three equal strips and arrange half the butter cubes over two-thirds of the dough.

___4___

Fold the outer two-thirds over, folding over the uncovered third last. Seal the edges with a rolling pin. Give the dough a quarter turn and roll it out again. Mark it into thirds and dot with the remaining butter cubes in the same way.

___5___

Chill the pastry for 20 minutes. Repeat the process of marking into thirds, folding over, giving a quarter turn and rolling out three times, chilling for 20 minutes in between each time. To make the filling, melt 4 tbsp butter and fry the shallots and garlic until soft but not browned. Add the remaining butter and the mushrooms and cook for 35–40 minutes. Drain off any excess liquid and stir in the remaining ingredients. Let cool. Preheat the oven to 450°F.

___6___

Divide the pastry in two. Roll out one half into a 9 in round, cutting around a plate to make a neat shape. Pile the filling into the center. Roll out the remaining pastry large enough to cover the base. Brush the edges of the base with water and then lay the second pastry circle on top. Press the edges together to seal and brush the top with a little beaten egg. Bake for 45 minutes, or until the pastry is risen, golden and flaky.

Turkey with Apples, Bay and Madeira

This casserole will win you many compliments without the worry of a complicated menu. The unusual apple garnish looks very attractive.

INGREDIENTS

1½ lb turkey breast fillets,
cut into ¾ in slices
salt and pepper
4 tbsp butter, plus another 1 tbsp
for the sliced apple garnish
4 tart apples, peeled and sliced
4 tbsp Madeira or cooking sherry,
plus another 2 tbsp for
the apple garnish
⅔ cup chicken stock
3 bay leaves
2 tsp cornstarch
⅔ cup heavy cream

Serves 4

1

Season the turkey, melt 2 tbsp the butter in a pan and fry the meat to seal it. Transfer to an ovenproof casserole. Preheat the oven to 350°F. Add the remaining 2 tbsps butter to the pan with two sliced apples, and cook gently for 1–2 minutes.

3

Blend the cornstarch with a little of the cream, then add the rest of the cream. Add this mixture to the casserole and return to the oven for 10 minutes to allow the sauce to thicken.

2

Add the Madeira, stock and bay leaves to the turkey and stir in. Simmer for another couple of minutes. Cover the casserole and bake for about 40 minutes.

4

To make the garnish, melt 1 tbsp butter in a pan and gently fry the apple slices. Add the remaining Madeira and set it alight. Once the flames have died down continue to fry the apple until it is lightly browned, and garnish the casserole with it.

Chicken with Sloe Gin and Juniper

Juniper is used in the manufacture of gin, and the reinforcement of the flavor by using both sloe gin and juniper is delicious. Sloe gin is easy to make, but can also be bought ready-made.

INGREDIENTS

2 tbsp butter
2 tbsp sunflower oil
8 chicken breast fillets
12 oz carrots, cooked
1 clove garlic, peeled and crushed
1 tbsp finely chopped parsley
¼ cup chicken stock
¼ cup red wine
¼ cup sloe gin
1 tsp crushed juniper berries
salt and pepper
1 bunch basil, to garnish

Serves 8

1

Melt the butter with the oil in a pan, and sauté the chicken until browned on all sides.

2

In a food processor, combine all the remaining ingredients except the watercress, and blend to a smooth purée. If the mixture seems too thick add a little more red wine or water until a thinner consistency is reached.

3

Put the chicken breasts in a pan, pour the sauce over the top and cool until the chicken is cooked through – about 15 minutes. Adjust the seasoning and serve garnished with chopped fresh basil.

Mushroom and Parsley Soup

*Thickened with bread, this rich mushroom soup will warm you up
on cold autumn days. It makes a terrific hearty lunch.*

INGREDIENTS

*6 tbsp unsalted butter
2 lb mushrooms, trimmed, wiped
and sliced
2 onions, coarsely chopped
2½ cups milk
8 slices white bread
4 tbsp chopped fresh parsley
1¼ cups heavy cream
salt and freshly ground
black pepper*

Serves 8

1

Melt the butter and sauté the mushrooms
and onions until soft but not colored –
about 10 minutes. Add the milk.

2

Tear the bread into pieces, drop them into
the soup and let the bread soak for
15 minutes. Purée the soup and return it to
the pan. Add the parsley, cream and seasoning.
Reheat, but do not allow the soup to boil.
Serve at once.

Thyme-roasted Onions

*These slowly roasted onions develop a delicious sweet flavor which is delicious
with roast meat. You could prepare parboiled new potatoes in the same way.*

INGREDIENTS

*5 tbsp olive oil
4 tbsp unsalted butter
2 lb small onions
2 tbsp chopped fresh thyme
salt and freshly ground
black pepper*

Serves 4

1

Preheat the oven to 425°F. Heat the oil
and butter in a large roasting pan. Add
the onions and toss them in the oil and
butter mixture.

2

Add the thyme and seasoning and roast for
45 minutes, basting regularly.

Duck and Chestnut Casserole

Serve this casserole with a mixture of mashed potatoes and celeriac,
to soak up the rich duck juices.

INGREDIENTS

4½ lb duck
3 tbsp olive oil
6 oz small onions
2 oz field mushrooms
2 oz shiitake mushrooms
1¼ cups dry red wine
such as Cabernet Sauvignon
1¼ cups beef stock,
fresh or canned
8 oz canned, peeled,
unsweetened chestnuts, drained
salt and freshly ground
black pepper

Serves 4–6

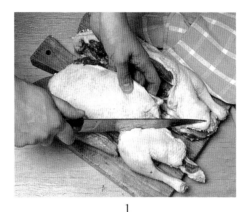

1

Cut the duck into eight pieces. Heat the oil
in a large frying pan and brown the duck
pieces. Remove from the frying pan.

2

Add the onions to the pan and brown them
well for 10 minutes.

3

Add the mushrooms and cook, stirring for
a few minutes more. Deglaze the pan with
the red wine and boil to reduce the
volume by half. Meanwhile, preheat the
oven to 350°F.

4

Pour the wine and the stock into a
casserole. Replace the duck, add the
chestnuts, season well and cook in the oven
for 1½ hours.

Cheese Scones

*These delicious scones make a good tea-time or brunch treat. They are best served
fresh and still slightly warm.*

INGREDIENTS

2 cups all-purpose flour
2¹/₂ tsp baking powder
¹/₂ tsp mustard powder
¹/₂ tsp salt
4 tbsp butter, chilled and cubed
3 oz Cheddar cheese, grated
²/₃ cup milk
1 egg, beaten

Makes 12

<u>1</u>

Preheat the oven to 450°F. Sift the flour,
baking powder, mustard powder and salt
into a mixing bowl. Add the butter and
rub it into the flour mixture until the
mixture resembles bread crumbs. Stir in
2 oz of the cheese.

<u>2</u>

Make a well in the center and add the milk
and egg. Mix gently and then turn the
dough out on to a lightly floured surface.
Roll it out and cut it into triangles or squares.
Brush lightly with milk and sprinkle with
the remaining cheese. Let rest for 15
minutes, then bake them for 15 minutes,
or until well risen.

Oatcakes

These are very simple to make and are an excellent addition to a cheese board.

INGREDIENTS

1²/₃ cups oatmeal
³/₄ cup all-purpose flour
¹/₄ tsp baking soda
tsp salt
2 tbsp Crisco
2 tbsp butter

Makes 24

<u>1</u>

Preheat the oven to 425°F. Place the
oatmeal, flour, soda and salt in a large bowl.
Gently melt the Crisco and butter together
in a pan.

<u>2</u>

Add the melted fat and enough boiling water
to make a soft dough. Turn out on to a
surface scattered with a little oatmeal.
Roll out the dough thinly and cut it into
circles. Bake the oatcakes on ungreased
baking sheets for 15 minutes, until crisp.

Blackberry Charlotte

A classic dessert, perfect for cold days. Serve with lightly whipped cream or homemade custard.

INGREDIENTS

5 tbsp unsalted butter
3 cups fresh white bread crumbs
4 tbsp brown sugar
4 tbsp maple syrup
finely grated rind and juice
of 2 lemons
2 oz walnut halves
1 lb blackberries
1 lb cooking apples, peeled,
cored and finely sliced
whipped cream or
custard, to serve

Serves 4

1

Preheat the oven to 350°F. Grease a 2 cup Pyrex dish with 1 tbsp of the butter. Melt the remaining butter and add the bread crumbs. Sauté them for 5–7 minutes, until the crumbs are slightly crisp and golden. Leave to cool slightly.

2

Place the sugar, syrup, lemon rind and juice in a small saucepan and gently warm them. Add the crumbs.

3

Process the walnuts until they are finely ground.

4

Arrange a thin layer of blackberries in the dish. Top with a thin layer of crumbs.

5

Add a thin layer of apple, topping it with another thin layer of crumbs. Repeat the process with another layer of blackberries, followed by a layer of crumbs. Continue until you have used up all the ingredients, finishing with a layer of crumbs.

The mixture should be piled well above the top edge of the dish, because it shrinks during cooking. Bake for 30 minutes, until the crumbs are golden and the fruit is soft.

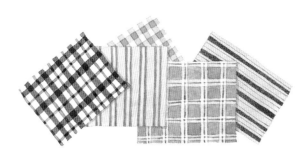

AUTUMN RECIPES

Poached Pears

Use a firm, sweet pear such as Bartlett or Anjou and serve warm.

INGREDIENTS

6 medium pears
*1¾ cups superfine
sugar*
3 tbsp honey
1 vanilla bean
2½ cups red wine
1 tsp whole cloves
3 in cinnamon stick
whipped cream to serve

Serves 4

1

Peel the pears but leave them whole,
keeping the stalks as well.

2

Put the sugar, honey, vanilla bean, wine,
cloves and cinnamon stick in a large pan.

3

Add the pears and poach until soft, about
30 minutes. When the pears are tender,
remove them with a slotted spoon and keep
them warm. Remove the vanilla bean, cloves
and cinnamon stick and boil the liquid
until it is reduced by half. Serve spooned
over the pears.

Steamed Ginger and Cinnamon Syrup Pudding

A traditional and comforting steamed pudding, best served with custard.

INGREDIENTS

9 tbsp softened butter
3 tbsp maple syrup
$\frac{1}{2}$ cup superfine sugar
2 eggs, lightly beaten
1 cup all-purpose flour
1 tsp baking powder
1 tsp ground cinnamon
1 oz preserved ginger,
finely chopped
2 tbsp milk
custard, to serve

Serves 4

1

Set a full steamer or saucepan of water on to boil. Lightly grease a 2½ cup pudding bowl with 1 tbsp butter. Place the maple syrup in the bowl.

2

Cream the remaining butter and sugar together until light and fluffy. Gradually add the eggs until the mixture is glossy. Sift the flour, baking powder and cinnamon together and fold them into the mixture, with the preserved ginger. Add the milk to make a soft, dropping consistency.

3

Spoon the batter into the bowl and smooth the top. Cover with a pleated piece of wax paper, to allow for expansion during cooking. Tie securely with string and steam for 1½–2 hours, making sure that the water level is kept topped up, to ensure a good flow of steam to cook the pudding. Turn the pudding out to serve it.

French Apple Tart

For added flavor, scatter some slivered almonds over the top of this classic tart.

INGREDIENTS

For the pastry
½ cup unsalted butter,
softened
4 tbsp vanilla sugar
1 egg
2 cups all-purpose flour

For the filling
4 tbsp unsalted butter
5 large tart apples, peeled, cored
and sliced
juice of ½ lemon
1¼ cups heavy cream
2 egg yolks
2 tbsp vanilla sugar
⅔ cup ground almonds,
toasted
2 tbsp slivered almonds, toasted,
to garnish

Serves 8

1

Place the butter and sugar in a food processor and process them well together. Add the egg and process to mix it in well.

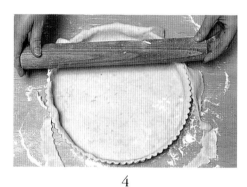

2

Add the flour and process till you have a soft dough. Wrap the dough in plastic wrap and chill it for 30 minutes.

3

Roll the pastry out on a lightly floured surface to about 9–10 in diameter.

4

Line a pie pan with the pastry and chill it for a further 30 minutes. Preheat the oven to 425°F and place a baking sheet in the oven to heat up. Line the pastry case with wax paper and baking beans and bake blind on the baking sheet for 10 minutes. Then remove the beans and paper and cook for a further 5 minutes.

5

Turn the oven down to 375°F. To make the filling, melt the butter in a frying pan and lightly sauté the apples for 5–7 minutes. Sprinkle the apples with lemon juice.

6

Beat the cream and egg yolks with the sugar. Stir in the toasted ground almonds. Arrange the apple slices on top of the warm pastry and pour over the cream mixture. Bake for 25 minutes, or until the cream is just about set – it tastes better if the cream is still slightly runny in the center. Serve hot or cold, scattered with slivered almonds.

Winter Recipes

....

*With the days growing shorter, we all need something
substantial and warming to keep out the cold.
Try roast beef with roasted peppers, or raised
country pie. Scotch pancakes or cranberry muffins
are a perfect fireside supper, and rich Christmas
pudding is the perfect way to round off the year.*

Roast Beef with Porcini and Sweet Bell Peppers

A substantial and warming dish for cold, dark evenings.

INGREDIENTS

3–3 ½ lb piece of sirloin
1 tbsp olive oil
1 lb small red bell peppers
4 oz mushrooms
6 oz thick-sliced pancetta
or bacon, cubed
2 tbsp all-purpose flour
⅔ cup full-bodied
red wine
1 ¼ cups beef stock
2 tbsp Marsala
2 tsp dried mixed herbs
salt and freshly ground
black pepper

Serves 8

1

Preheat the oven to 375°F. Season the meat
well. Heat the olive oil in a large frying pan.
When very hot, brown the meat on all sides.
Place in a large roasting pan and cook
for 1 ¼ hours.

2

Put the red peppers in the oven to roast for
20 minutes, if small ones are available, or
45 minutes if large ones are used.

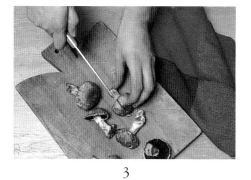

3

Near the end of the meat's cooking time,
prepare the gravy. Coarsely chop the
mushroom caps and stems.

4

Heat the frying pan again and add the
pancetta or bacon. Cook until the fat runs
freely from the meat. Add the flour and cook
for a few minutes until browned.

5

Gradually stir in the red wine and the stock.
Bring to a boil, stirring. Lower the heat
and add the Marsala, herbs and seasoning.

6

Add the mushrooms to the pan and heat
through. Remove the sirloin from the oven
and leave to stand for 10 minutes before
carving it. Serve with the roasted peppers
and the hot gravy.

Bacon and Lentil Soup

Serve this hearty soup with chunks of warm, crusty bread.

INGREDIENTS

*1 lb thick-sliced bacon,
cubed
1 onion, coarsely chopped
1 small turnip, coarsely chopped
1 celery stalk, chopped
1 carrot, sliced
1 potato, peeled and
coarsely chopped
½ cup lentils
1 bouquet garni
freshly ground black pepper*

Serves 4

1

Heat a large pan and add the bacon. Cook for
a few minutes, allowing the fat to run out.

2

Add all the vegetables and cook for
4 minutes.

3

Add the lentils, bouquet garni, seasoning
and enough water to cover. Bring to a boil
and simmer for 1 hour, or until the lentils
are tender.

Creamy Layered Potatoes

Cook the potatoes on top of the stove first to help the dish to bake more quickly.

INGREDIENTS

3–3½ lb large potatoes, peeled
and sliced
2 large onions, sliced
6 tbsp unsalted butter
1¼ cups heavy cream
salt and freshly ground
black pepper

Serves 6

1

Preheat the oven to 400°F. Blanch the sliced
potatoes for 2 minutes, and drain well.

2

Place the potatoes, onions, butter and cream
in a pan, stir well and cook for about
15 minutes. Transfer to a large ovenproof
dish, season well and bake for 1 hour, until
the potatoes are tender.

Traditional Beef Stew and Dumplings

This dish can cook in the oven while you go for a wintery walk to work up an appetite.

INGREDIENTS

1 tbsp all-purpose flour
2½ lb stewing beef,
cubed
2 tbsp olive oil
2 large onions, sliced
1 lb carrots, sliced
½ pint / 1¼ cups Guinness
or dark beer
3 bay leaves
2 tsp brown sugar
3 fresh thyme sprigs
1 tsp cider vinegar
salt and freshly ground
black pepper

For the dumplings
½ cup chopped Crisco
2 cups self-rising
flour
2 tbsp chopped mixed
fresh herbs
about ⅔ cup water

Serves 6

1

Preheat the oven to 325°F. Season the flour and sprinkle over the meat, tossing to coat.

2

Heat the oil in a large casserole and lightly sauté the onions and carrots. Remove the vegetables with a slotted spoon and reserve them.

3

Brown the meat well in batches in the casserole.

4

Return all the vegetables to the casserole and add any leftover seasoned flour. Add the Guinness or beer, bay leaves, sugar and thyme. Bring the liquid to a boil and then transfer to the oven.

6

Form the dough into small balls with floured hands. Add the cider vinegar to the meat and spoon the dumplings on top. Cook for a further 20 minutes, until the dumplings have cooked through and serve hot.

5

After the meat has been cooking for 1 hour and 40 minutes, make the dumplings. Mix the Crisco and flour together. Add enough water to make a soft, sticky dough.

Country Pie

A classic raised pie. It takes quite a long time to make,
but is a perfect winter treat.

INGREDIENTS

1 small duck
1 small chicken
12 oz pork belly, minced
1 egg, lightly beaten
2 shallots, finely chopped
½ tsp ground cinnamon
½ tsp grated nutmeg
1 tsp Worcestershire sauce
finely grated rind of 1 lemon
½ tsp freshly ground black pepper
⅔ cup red wine
6 oz ham, cut into cubes
salt and freshly ground
black pepper

For the aspic
all the meat bones and trimmings
2 carrots
1 onion
2 celery stalks
1 tbsp red wine
1 bay leaf
1 whole clove
1 packet of gelatin
(about 1 oz)

For the pastry
1 cup Crisco
1¼ cups boiling water
6 cups all-purpose flour
1 egg, lightly beaten with a
pinch of salt

Serves 12

1

Cut as much meat from the raw duck and
chicken as possible, removing the skin and
sinews. Cut the duck and chicken breasts
into cubes and set them aside.

2

Mix the rest of the duck and chicken meat
with the minced pork, egg, shallots, spices,
Worcestershire sauce, lemon rind and salt
and pepper. Add the red wine and leave for
about 15 minutes for the flavors to develop.

3

To make the aspic, place the meat bones and
trimmings, carrots, onion, celery, wine, bay
leaf and clove in a large pan and cover with
12½ cups of water. Bring to a boil,
skimming off any scum, and simmer
gently for 2½ hours.

4

To make the pastry, place the fat and water
in a pan and bring to a boil. Sift the flour
with a pinch of salt into a bowl and pour on
the hot liquid. Mix with a wooden spoon,
and, when the dough is cool enough to
handle, knead it well and let it sit in a warm
place, covered with a cloth, for 20–30
minutes or until you are ready to use it.
Preheat the oven to 400°F.

5

Grease a 10 in loose-based deep cake pan. Roll out about two-thirds of the pastry thinly enough to line the cake pan. Make sure there are no holes and allow enough pastry to leave a little hanging over the top. Fill the pie with a layer of half the minced-pork mixture; then top this with a layer of the cubed duck and chicken breast-meat and cubes of ham. Top with the remaining minced pork. Brush the overhanging edges of pastry with water and cover with the remaining rolled-out pastry. Seal the edges well. Make two large holes in the top and decorate with any pastry trimmings.

6

Bake the pie for 30 minutes. Brush the top with the egg and salt mixture. Turn down the oven to 350°F. After 30 minutes loosely cover the pie with foil to prevent the top getting too brown, and bake it for a further 1 hour.

7

Strain the stock after 2½ hours. Let it cool and remove the solidified layer of fat from the surface. Measure 2½ cups of stock. Heat it gently to just below boiling point and whisk the gelatin into it until no lumps are left. Add the remaining strained stock and leave to cool.

8

When the pie is cool, place a funnel through one of the holes and pour in as much of the stock as possible, letting it come up to the holes in the crust. Leave to set for at least 24 hours before slicing and serving.

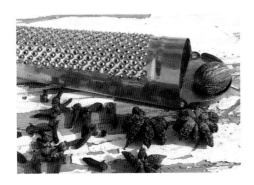

Leek and Onion Tart

This unusual recipe isn't a normal tart with pastry, but an all-in-one savory slice that is excellent served as an accompaniment to roast meat.

INGREDIENTS

4 tbsp unsalted butter
12 oz leeks, sliced thinly
2 cups self-rising flour
½ cup Crisco
⅔ cup water
salt and freshly ground black pepper

Serves 4

1

Preheat the oven to 400°F. Melt the butter in a pan and sauté the leeks until soft. Season well.

2

Mix the flour, fat and water together in a bowl to make a soft but sticky dough. Mix into the leek mixture in the pan. Place in a greased shallow ovenproof dish and bake for 30 minutes, or until brown and crispy. Serve sliced, as a vegetable accompaniment.

Orange Shortbread Fingers

*These are a real tea-time treat. The fingers will keep in an airtight tin
for up to two weeks.*

*½ cup unsalted butter,
softened
4 tbsp superfine sugar,
plus a little extra
finely grated rind of 2 oranges
1½ cups all-purpose flour*

Makes 18

1

Preheat the oven to 375°F. Beat the butter
and sugar together until they are soft and
creamy. Beat in the orange rind.

2

Gradually add the flour and gently pull the
dough together to form a soft ball. Roll the
dough out on a lightly floured surface until
about ½ in thick. Cut it into fingers,
sprinkle over a little extra superfine sugar,
prick with a fork and bake for about
20 minutes, or until the fingers are a
light golden color.

Cranberry Muffins

A tea or breakfast dish that is not too sweet.

INGREDIENTS

3 cups all-purpose flour
1 tsp baking powder
pinch of salt
½ cup superfine sugar
2 eggs
⅔ cup milk
4 tbsp corn oil
finely grated rind of 1 orange
5 oz cranberries

Makes 12

1

Preheat the oven to 375°F. Line a muffin pan with paper cases. Mix the flour, baking powder, salt and superfine sugar together.

2

Lightly beat the eggs with the milk and oil. Add them to the dry ingredients and blend to make a smooth batter. Stir in the orange rind and cranberries. Divide the mixture between the muffin cases and bake for 25 minutes until risen and golden. Let cool in the pan for a few minutes, and serve warm or cold.

Country Pancakes

Serve these hot with butter and maple syrup or jam.

INGREDIENTS

2 cups self-rising flour
4 tbsp superfine sugar
4 tbsp butter, melted
1 egg
1¼ cups milk
1 tbsp corn oil or margarine

Makes 24

1

Mix the flour and sugar together. Add the melted butter and egg with two-thirds of the milk. Mix to a smooth batter – it should be thin enough to find its own level.

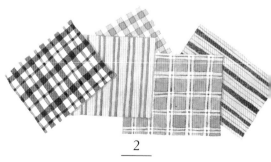

2

Heat a griddle or a heavy-based frying pan and wipe it with a little oil or margarine. When hot, drop spoonfuls of the mixture on to the hot griddle or pan. When bubbles come to the surface of the pancakes, flip them over to cook until golden on the other side. Keep the pancakes warm wrapped in a dish towel while cooking the rest of the mixture. Serve as soon as possible.

Christmas Pudding

The classic Christmas dessert. Wrap it in cheesecloth and store it in an airtight container for up to a year for the flavors to develop.

INGREDIENTS

*1 cup all-purpose flour
pinch of salt
1 tsp ground allspice
½ tsp ground cinnamon
¼ tsp freshly grated nutmeg
1 cup grated hard Crisco
1 apple, grated
2 cups fresh white
bread crumbs
1⅞ cups soft brown
sugar
2 oz slivered almonds
1½ cups seedless raisins
1½ cups currants
1½ cups golden raisins
4 oz ready-to-eat dried
apricots
¾ cup chopped mixed
citrus peel
finely grated rind and juice
of 1 lemon
2 tbsp molasses
3 eggs
1¼ cups milk
2 tbsp rum*

Serves 8

1

Sift the flour, salt and spices into
a large bowl.

2

Add the Crisco, apple and other dry
ingredients, including the grated
lemon rind.

3

Heat the molasses until warm and runny
and pour into the dry ingredients.

4

Mix together the eggs, milk, rum
and lemon juice.

5

Stir the liquid into the dry mixture.

6

Spoon the mixture into two 5 cup bowls.
Wrap the puddings with pieces of wax paper,
pleated to allow for expansion, and tie with
string. Steam the puddings in a steamer or
saucepan of boiling water. Each pudding
needs 10 hours' cooking and 3 hours'
reheating. Remember to keep the water level
topped up to keep the pans from boiling dry.
Serve decorated with holly.

Gifts from the Pantry

Make the most of seasonal fruits and vegetables,
by making jams, jellies and preserves to enjoy
the year round, or to give as gifts.
Country favorites include strawberry jam,
apple and mint jelly, or piccalilli.

Apple and Mint Jelly

This jelly is delicious served with garden peas, as well as the more traditional rich roasted meat such as lamb.

INGREDIENTS

2 lb cooking apples
granulated sugar
3 tbsp chopped fresh mint

Makes 3 × 1 lb jars

1

Chop the apples coarsely and put them in a preserving pan.

2

Add enough water to cover. Simmer until the fruit is soft.

3

Pour through a jelly bag, allowing it to drip overnight. Do not squeeze the bag or the jelly will become cloudy.

4

Measure the amount of juice. To every 2½ cups of juice, add 2¾ cups granulated sugar.

5

Place the juice and sugar in a large pan and heat gently. Dissolve the sugar and then bring to a boil. Test for setting, by pouring about 1 tbsp into a saucer and leaving to cool slightly. If a wrinkle forms on the surface when pushed with a fingertip, the jelly will set. When a set is reached, leave to cool.

6

Stir in the mint and pour into sterilized jars. Seal each jar with a waxed disc and a tightly fitting plastic top. Store in a cool, dark place. The jelly will keep unopened for up to a year. Once opened, keep in the fridge and consume within a week.

Lemon and Lime Curd

Serve this creamy, tangy spread with toast or muffins,
instead of jam, for a delightful change.

INGREDIENTS

½ cup unsalted butter	grated rind and juice of 2 lemons
3 eggs	grated rind and juice of 2 limes
	1 ⅛ cups superfine sugar

Makes 2 × 1 lb jars

1

Set a heatproof mixing bowl over a large pan
of simmering water. Add the butter.

2

Lightly beat the eggs and add them
to the butter.

3

Add the lemon and lime rinds and juices,
then add the sugar.

4

Stir the mixture constantly until it thickens.
Pour into sterilized jars. Seal each jar with a
waxed disc and a tightly fitting plastic top.
Store in a cool, dark place. The curd will
keep unopened for up to a month.
Once opened, keep in the fridge and
consume within a week.

Poached Spiced Plums in Brandy

Canning spiced fruit is a great way to preserve summer flavors for eating in winter. Serve these with whipped cream as a dessert.

INGREDIENTS

2 1/2 cups brandy
rind of 1 lemon, peeled in a long strip
1 2/3 cups superfine sugar
1 cinnamon stick
2 lb fresh plums

Makes 2 lb

1

Put the brandy, lemon rind, sugar and cinnamon stick in a large pan and heat gently to dissolve the sugar. Add the plums and poach for 15 minutes, or until soft. Remove with a slotted spoon.

2

Reduce the syrup by a third by rapid boiling. Strain it over the plums. Pack the plums in large sterilized jars. Seal tightly and store for up to 6 months in a cool, dark place.

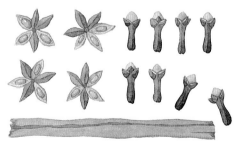

Spiced Pickled Pears

These delicious pears are the perfect accompaniment for cooked ham
or cold meat salads.

2 lb pears
2½ cups white-wine
vinegar
1⅛ cups superfine sugar
1 cinnamon stick
5 star anise
10 whole cloves

Makes 2 lb

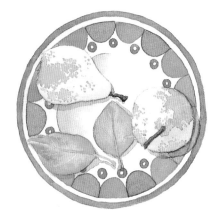

1

Peel the pears, keeping them whole
and leaving on the stalks. Heat the vinegar
and sugar together until the sugar has melted.
Pour over the pears and poach for 15 minutes.

2

Add the cinnamon, star anise and cloves
and simmer for 10 minutes. Remove the
pears and pack tightly into sterilized jars.
Simmer the syrup for a further 15 minutes
and pour it over the pears. Seal the jars
tightly and store in a cool, dark place. The
pears will keep for up to a year unopened.
Once opened, store in the fridge and
consume within a week.

Tomato Chutney

This spicy chutney is delicious with a selection of cheeses and biscuits,
or with cold meats.

INGREDIENTS

2 lb tomatoes, skinned   1 ⅛ cups superfine sugar
1 ⅓ cups raisins   2 ½ cups cider
8 oz onions, chopped   vinegar

Makes 4 × 1 lb jars

1

Chop the tomatoes coarsely. Put them in
a preserving pan.

2

Add the raisins, onions and sugar.

3

Pour over the vinegar. Bring to a boil
and let it simmer for 2 hours, uncovered.
Pot into sterilized jars. Seal with a waxed disc
and cover with a tightly fitting plastic
top. Store in a cool, dark place. The chutney
will keep unopened for up to a year. Once
opened, store in the fridge and consume
within a week.

Strawberry Jam

This classic recipe is always popular. Make sure the jam is allowed to cool before pouring into jars so the fruit doesn't float to the top.

3–3 ½ lb strawberries
juice of ½ lemon
3–3 ½ lb granulated sugar

Makes about 5 lb

1

Hull the strawberries.

2

Put the strawberries in a pan with the lemon juice. Mash a few of the strawberries. Let the fruit simmer for 20 minutes or until softened.

3

Add the sugar and let it dissolve slowly over a gentle heat. Then let the jam boil rapidly until a setting point is reached.

4

Let stand until the strawberries are well distributed through the jam. Pack into sterilized jars. Seal each jar with a waxed disc and cover with a tightly fitting plastic top. Store in a cool dark place. The jam may be kept unopened for up to a year. Once opened, keep in the fridge and consume within a week.

Three-fruit Marmalade

Homemade marmalade may be time-consuming but the results are incomparably better than storebought varieties.

INGREDIENTS

12 oz oranges
12 oz lemons
1½ lb grapefruit
10¼ cups water
6 lb granulated sugar

Makes 6 × 1 lb jars

1

Rinse the fruit and dry them.

2

Put the fruit in a preserving pan. Add the water and let it simmer for about 2 hours.

3

Quarter the fruit, remove the pulp and add it to the pan with the cooking liquid.

4

Cut the rinds into slivers, and add to the pan. Add the sugar. Gently heat until the sugar has dissolved. Bring to a boil and cook until a setting point is reached. Let stand for 1 hour to allow the peel to settle. Pour into sterilized jars. Seal each jar with a waxed disc and a tightly fitting plastic top. Store in a cool, dark place.

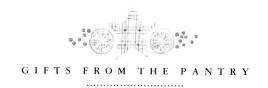

Piccalilli

The piquancy of this relish partners well with sausages, bacon or ham.

INGREDIENTS

1½ lb cauliflower	1 tsp dry mustard powder
1 lb small onions	2 tsp corn starch
12 oz green beans	2½ cups vinegar
1 tsp ground turmeric	

Makes 3 × 1 lb jars

1

Cut the cauliflower into tiny florets.

2

Peel the onions and top and tail
the green beans.

3

In a small saucepan, measure in the turmeric,
mustard powder and corn starch, and pour
over the vinegar. Stir well and simmer
for 10 minutes.

4

Pour the vinegar mixture over the vegetables
in a pan, mix well and simmer
for 45 minutes.

5

Pour into sterilized jars. Seal each jar with a
waxed disc and a tightly fitting plastic
top. Store in a cool dark place. The piccalilli
will keep unopened for up to a year. Once
opened store in the fridge and consume
within a week.

Rosemary-flavored Oil

This pungent oil is ideal drizzled over meat or vegetables before grilling.

INGREDIENTS

2½ cups olive oil
5 fresh rosemary sprigs

Makes 2½ cups

1

Heat the oil until warm but not too hot.

2

Add four rosemary sprigs and heat gently.
Put the reserved rosemary sprig in a clean
bottle. Strain the oil, pour in the bottle and
seal tightly. Allow to cool and store in a
cool, dark place. Use within a week.

Thyme-flavored Vinegar

This vinegar is delicious sprinkled over salmon intended for poaching.

INGREDIENTS

*2½ cups white-wine
vinegar*
5 fresh thyme sprigs
3 garlic cloves, peeled

Makes 2½ cups

1

Warm the vinegar.

2

Add four thyme sprigs and the garlic and
heat gently. Put the reserved thyme sprig in
a clean bottle, strain the vinegar, and add to
the bottle. Seal tightly, allow to cool and
store in a cool, dark place. The vinegar
may be kept unopened for up to 3 months.

Index